# Z is for Zookeeper

## A Zoo Alphabet

Written by Marie & Roland Smith and Illustrated by Henry Cole

## Sleeping Bear Press

310 North Main Street, Suite 300
Chelsea, MI 48118
www.sleepingbearpress.com

**THOMSON**
★
**GALE**

© 2005 Thomson Gale, a part of the Thomson Corporation.

Thomson, Star Logo and Sleeping Bear Press are trademarks
and Gale is a registered trademark used herein under license.

Printed and bound in Canada.

10 9 8 7 6 5 4 3 2 1

Library of Congress Cataloging-in-Publication Data

Smith, Marie, 1951-
Z is for zookeeper : a zoo alphabet / written by Marie and Roland Smith ;
illustrated by Henry Cole.
p. cm.
Summary: "An A-Z pictorial for children all about zookeepers and their role
at the zoo. Letter topics include animals, brooms, disinfectant, veterinarian,
keys, and locks. Topics are introduced with poems accompanied by expository
text to provide detailed information"—Provided by publisher.
ISBN 1-58536-158-5
1. Zoos—Juvenile literature. 2. English language—Alphabet—Juvenile literature.
I. Smith, Roland, 1951- II. Cole, Henry, 1955- III. Title.

QL76.S628 2005
590.73—dc22                    2004027302

*For our three little monkeys—John, Will, and Jack.*

*With love,*
AHNA & GRAMPS

\*

*With thanks to Dan, Erin, Linda, Tina, Brian,*
*and Marilyn at the National Zoo.*

HENRY

Where do zoo animals come from? Most of the animals you see in the zoo were born in the zoo. The days of going out into the wild and catching animals to exhibit in a zoo are long gone. Many of the animals kept in zoos are not there just for our entertainment. They are there because it is no longer safe for them in the wild and they are in danger of becoming extinct.

Wilderness areas where animals can live in peace are disappearing.

Today zoos are helping preserve animals by breeding rare and endangered species and sometimes finding areas to reintroduce these animals back into the wild.

This important work starts with the zookeeper.

A is for the Animals
that live in the zoo.
Caring for creatures
is what zookeepers do.

**B** is for Brooms.
Sweeping is one way
zookeepers clean
each and every day.

One of the zookeeper's responsibilities is keeping the animal habitats clean. Cleaning is necessary to keep animals healthy.

In the wild when an animal defecates, or poops, it can walk away from it. In a zoo, where animals are confined, they can't walk away—at least not very far. This is why zookeepers spend a good deal of their day cleaning up after the animals.

Most of the cleaning takes place early in the morning before the zoo opens. Zookeepers use brooms, shovels, rakes, pooper-scoopers, and other equipment to pick up animal droppings.

If an animal can't walk away from its poop, the zookeeper makes sure the poop is walked away from the animal!

C is for the Cats
with a terrifying roar.
When zookeepers first hear it
they jump off the floor!

Cats are in the *Felidae* family—a Latin word meaning "catlike." Cats come in many different sizes, colors, and patterns. The biggest is the tiger from Asia, weighing 350 to 600 pounds (158.8 to 272.2 kg). The tiger has black vertical stripes against golden fur. These stripes help to camouflage the animal while it hunts in the forest. Lions come in a close second at 260 to 550 pounds (117.9 to 249.5 kg). Adult lions have tan-colored fur without spots or stripes. They blend in well with the grassy African savanna where they live and hunt.

There are 29 species of small wildcats throughout the world. The smallest is the rusty spotted cat found in southern India. It's very tiny, weighing only 2 to 4.5 pounds (.91 to 2.0 kg).

A lion may be smaller than a tiger, but its roar is much louder than its larger striped cousin. You can hear a lion's roar from miles away. Zookeepers don't go inside the exhibit with the big cats, but they have to get close to feed them their meat. Hearing a lion roar from inches away is an experience zookeepers never forget.

It is not only important to clean what you see in the animal exhibit, but it is also important to clean the things you can't see. Zookeepers wash away microscopic bacteria and germs that may make an animal sick. Even though they use special soaps and disinfectants safe for the animals, zookeepers carefully rinse the exhibit after using disinfectants to make sure all the soap is gone. Zookeepers don't like to take chances that anything will harm their animals. Most of the time animals are kept away while the zookeeper cleans. This helps keep both the animal and the zookeeper safe.

**D** is also for director. A director is the person who is in charge of the whole zoo. Zoos also have people called curators. There may be a mammal curator in charge of all the mammals, or a bird curator in charge of all the birds. Zookeepers answer directly to the curator in charge of their section of the zoo.

**D** is for Disinfectants
that zookeepers pour,
killing the germs
that live on the floor.

Elephants, rhinoceros, and hippopotamus are found in a group of animals called *pachyderms*. This word means "thick-skinned."

Most zoo animals wear their claws, talons, or toenails down naturally. But not elephants. To keep the elephants' feet healthy, zookeepers have to trim and file their toenails. This is a big job. One zookeeper has to keep the elephant steady while the other zookeeper does the pachyderm pedicure.

There are two kinds of elephants, African and Asian. To tell the difference, look at their ears. African elephants have ears shaped like the continent of Africa. Asian elephants (sometimes called Indian elephants) have ears shaped like the country of India.

Another way to tell the difference is to look at the elephant's toenails. African elephants usually have four toenails on their front feet and three on their back feet. Asian elephants have five toenails on their front feet and four on their back feet.

**E** is for Elephants.
Zookeepers check their toes—
keeping them clipped
as each nail grows.

F is for Flight.
Look at the sky.
Zookeepers care for
creatures that fly.

Birds are often kept together in large flight cages called aviaries. These exhibits are very natural, with trees, plants, ponds, and streams. In some zoos, visitors are allowed inside the aviary so they can see the birds up close without barriers.

Aviaries are beautiful, and good for the birds, but they are difficult to manage. It takes a lot of time to get all those branches and leaves clean. Zoo gardeners help the zookeepers take care of the plants. Spare plants are kept in greenhouses and rotated in and out of the aviary, usually on a weekly basis.

Because the birds are free to fly wherever they want, they are also free to steal food from each other. This makes added work for zookeepers who have to make sure all the birds get the food they need.

**F** is also for flightless. All birds have wings, but not all birds can fly. Flightless birds, called *ratites*, use their powerful legs to get around. These birds include kiwis, ostriches, emus, and cassowaries.

G g

Animals sometimes need to be transported between zoos. Small animals like monkeys and birds are usually put into a kennel and flown to their new home in the cargo hold of a commercial jet. Big cats like lions and tigers are usually put into secure crates and are driven to their destination. Elephants are walked into the back of semitrailers and driven as well. But how do you move a really tall animal?

An adult giraffe can weigh 3,000 pounds (1360.8 kg) and stand 18 feet (5.5 m) tall. No truck or airplane is tall enough to hold a giraffe. When a giraffe is transported it is put into an open truck with its neck and head sticking out of a crate. The weather has to be perfect. Not too cold, not too hot. And the route the truck driver takes has to be planned very carefully. He cannot drive under low overpasses or bridges. Giraffes can't duck their heads while traveling 55 miles (88.5 km) per hour!

**G** is for Giraffes
with an interesting view—
traveling through towns
from zoo to zoo.

If you look toward the back of most zoo exhibits you will see doors. Behind these doors are animal holding areas. These are used as sleeping areas for animals at night. These are also where some animals are held while the zookeepers clean the exhibit. When the zookeeper is done cleaning the outside exhibit she lets the animals out, then cleans the holding area so it's ready for the next day.

Holding areas are also used for animals when they get sick, and as dens for giving birth.

H is for Holding—
a cage out of sight.
Zookeepers use these
for animals at night.

# I i

**I** is for Incubator.
Eggs in a batch
are kept warm and safe
so babies can hatch.

Most of the eggs laid in the zoo are hatched in incubators. An incubator is a special machine that keeps eggs at the right temperature and humidity. Eggs are taken from the nest to prevent them from being broken by the mother or other animals. When the baby hatches it is hand-raised in the zoo nursery.

When we think of eggs we usually think of birds. But other animals lay eggs too. Turtles, snakes, lizards, and alligators all lay eggs to have their young.

Human incubators are also used for newborn primates, small mammals, and birds. Incubators are ideal because the temperature and humidity can be controlled and the baby can be observed without having to open the cage.

J is for Joeys—
    in mother's pouch they hide.
Zookeepers first see them
    with eyes open wide.

Baby kangaroos are called joeys. When they are born they are about the size of a bumblebee, and blind. Even so, it takes them only three minutes to climb up their mother's fur (in a swimming motion) and disappear over the lip of the pouch. To find its way, the joey uses its sense of smell and a built-in gravity sensor in the inner ear. The sensor tells the joey which way is up and down. Inside the pouch the joey latches onto its mother's nipple. And there it stays, taking nourishment and getting bigger and bigger everyday.

The joey doesn't take its first peek outside the pouch until it's five or six months old. Soon after this it starts to leave the pouch for short periods of time to socialize and play with other kangaroos. If the joey gets scared it hops back into its mother's pouch.

Zookeepers can usually tell when a kangaroo is about to give birth. Two days before, the mother begins to clean her pouch, getting its built-in nursery ready for the new baby.

J j

At a zoo, locks are used to keep animals in and unauthorized people out.

There are many locks in a zoo, but most of them open with just one key. This way zookeepers don't have to carry too many keys. But if a zookeeper loses a key, all the locks the key opens have to be changed. This can cost thousands of dollars! Because of this, zookeepers are very careful about their keys.

Locks and keys are always on the zoo-keeper's mind, even at night. Sometimes, after the zookeeper has gone to sleep, they have "lock dreams." They wake up in the middle of the night wondering if they locked all the locks before going home. If they have doubts they might jump out of bed and drive all the way to the zoo to make sure. Most of the time the lock they thought was unlocked is locked! But you can't be too careful.

"Don't lose your keys,"
all zookeepers say.
Changing locks is expensive.
Key starts with the letter K.

L is for Locks
zookeepers call red.
These locks make sure
animals are safe in bed.

When a zookeeper cleans the exhibit of a potentially dangerous animal, like a lion or polar bear, he locks the animals inside the holding area with a special lock called a red lock or safety lock. They are called "red" because these special locks are often painted the color red. This way people know that the animal is to stay in its holding area until the zookeeper lets it out.

No one but the zookeeper cleaning the exhibit has the key to a red lock. Not even the zoo director! This prevents someone from coming along and accidentally letting the animals back into their exhibit when the zookeeper is working in the exhibit.

Ll

Monkeys are very intelligent animals, and extremely curious. They need to be kept in a natural exhibit with a lot to do—otherwise they get bored.

Zookeepers hide food in the exhibit to keep the monkeys busy. Fruits, vegetables, monkey-chow biscuits, seeds, nuts, and even insects are hidden.

Monkeys love to eat crickets. In some zoos, zookeepers bury long sections of plastic pipe underground. In the morning the zookeeper lets a handful of crickets loose. The crickets crawl down the pipes throughout the day. The monkeys never know when or where the cricket will come out. This keeps them alert and busy.

Zookeepers also put balls, rope swings, and other toys in the exhibit for the monkeys to play with.

Orangutan, pigmy chimpanzee, and the beautiful little golden lion tamarin are all part of a program called the Species Survival Plan® managed by the American Zoo & Aquarium Association (AZA). Zoos are trying to save these and other endangered species from extinction.

M is for Monkeys.
They look like kin.
As if they should be out,
rather than in.

The best zoo nursery is an empty zoo nursery. Zookeepers would prefer to have a baby's natural mother raise it. But sometimes zoo mothers get sick; sometimes zoo babies get sick, and they have to be hand-raised in the nursery.

Baby animals are delicate and need a lot of nurturing to keep them healthy. Zookeepers, along with the zoo nutritionist and veterinarian, develop special formulas to feed the baby animals.

Just like human babies, zoo babies must be fed every few hours. This means at least one zookeeper has to be in the nursery 24 hours a day, 7 days a week to give babies the care they need.

When a baby hatches or is born it forms an emotional bond with the humans who are feeding and caring for it. Because of this, the hatchling might think it's a person. This is called imprinting. This can cause problems later when the hatchling is put back with animals of its own kind. To lessen the effects of imprinting, zookeepers sometimes feed the hatchling with puppets that look like its real mother.

N is for Nursery
where zoo babies stay.
Zookeepers take care of them
all night and all day.

Zookeepers Observe.
That starts with the letter O.
Zookeepers watch carefully
for things they need to know.

Zookeepers spend a good part of their day watching the animals under their care.

It's important to get to know your animals, and the only way to do this is to spend time watching them. By observing the animals, and writing down what they see, zookeepers are often able to pick up problems before they become serious.

They watch how the animal moves. Is it limping? They watch how the animal eats. Is it getting enough food and water? They watch how the animals interact. Are they getting along? Is there any sign of aggression between them? Is there anything the zookeeper can do to make their exhibit better?

These and other questions are critical and need to be answered every day.

**P** is for Penguins
jumping in the pool.
A zookeeper's job
is keeping them cool.

There are 17 different species of penguins. All of them are found in the southern hemisphere. In the wild they live in a cold and pure environment with very few germs and virtually no disease. Because of this, penguins are housed in a special building at the zoo. The air they breathe and chilled water they swim in is filtered to keep out harmful bacteria and germs.

Penguins are social animals and are kept in large groups called colonies. Each one is marked with different colored tags so zookeepers can tell them apart.

It takes at least two zookeepers to feed a colony of penguins. One to feed and another to keep track and write down how many fish each penguin eats.

**Q** is for Quarantine.
    When animals are new,
here they are kept
        before entering the zoo.

All new animals coming into the zoo are kept by themselves in a special area called quarantine. Ideally, the quarantine area is off the zoo grounds, away from all the other animals.

The reason new animals are kept separate is to make sure they don't have a disease that might be passed onto the healthy animals in the zoo. Quarantine periods vary, depending on the animal and zoo. But it wouldn't be unusual for an animal to remain in quarantine for a month before it was allowed into the zoo.

The quarantine zookeeper has to be very careful about spreading germs. He washes his hands before and after going into a quarantined animal cage. He also has to step into footbaths with special germ-killing soap.

In some zoos the zookeepers in charge of quarantine are quarantined themselves! On the days they work quarantine, they aren't allowed into the zoo where the other animals are kept.

q

Q

**R** is for Records
zookeepers must keep
on everything animals do
throughout the week.

Record keeping is another important part of a zookeeper's job. Before going home, zookeepers sit at their desks and write down everything that happened to their animals that day.

How much food did they eat? Did they take their medications and vitamins? Are the animals getting along with each other?

The answer to these and other questions are very important to the health of zoo animals.

When zookeepers want to find out what happened to their animals on their days off, all they have to do is read the daily record their relief keeper kept. It tells them everything they need to know.

When an animal goes to another zoo, its records go with it. This helps the new zookeeper take better care of the animal.

**S** is for Snake,
on mice they exist.
A zookeeper who cares for them
is a herpetologist.

Snakes come in all sizes. The largest snake in the world is the anaconda from South America, which can reach a length of more than 30 feet (9.1 m). One of the smallest is the Texas blind—an adult is only six inches (15.2 cm) long.

Snakes are commonly thought to be cold-blooded, but this is not exactly true. They are actually "ectothermic," which means that their bodies cannot produce heat. Zookeepers make sure snakes have warm spots in their cages so the snakes can regulate their own temperature.

Most snakes eat rodents, like rats and mice. They require much less food than a warm-blooded animal. In fact, a dog can eat more food in a single meal than a rattlesnake eats in an entire year!

Some people don't like to watch snakes eat, so zookeepers feed them when the public is not there, or cover the cage so nobody can see them eating. Another reason for not feeding a snake in public is that some snakes will refuse to eat if they know they are being watched.

Ss

# T t

T is for Trucks
that deliver the feed—
all kinds of food
that the animals need.

Every zoo exhibit has a small kitchen or food prep area where zookeepers prepare the food to feed their animals. A huge central kitchen, called the commissary, services these small kitchens.

This is where all the fruits, vegetables, meat, and grain are stored. Every morning the commissary keeper lays out the food for all the animals in the zoo. This food is delivered by truck to the animal areas before the zookeepers come to work.

What the animals eat is carefully controlled by the zoo nutritionist, with help from the zookeeper and veterinarian. It's the nutritionist's job to make sure the animals get a healthy and balanced diet.

**U** is for Uniforms
zookeepers wear doing tasks.
If visitors have questions
they know who to ask.

Zookeepers wear uniforms and nametags so visitors know who they are. They have winter uniforms to keep them warm and summer uniforms to keep them cool.

Zookeepers usually wear boots to protect their feet from getting stepped on. They usually carry a pocketknife for cutting up fruits and vegetables or the strings around hay bales. Most zookeepers also carry radios so they can stay in touch with other zookeepers, the veterinarian, and the curator.

You won't see a zookeeper wearing much in the way of jewelry. Animals, especially monkeys, like to grab shiny things. That can be dangerous for the zookeeper and rough on the jewelry.

If you have a question about an animal, look for the zookeeper. If she isn't busy, she's happy to answer questions and enjoys talking about the animals she cares for.

u
U

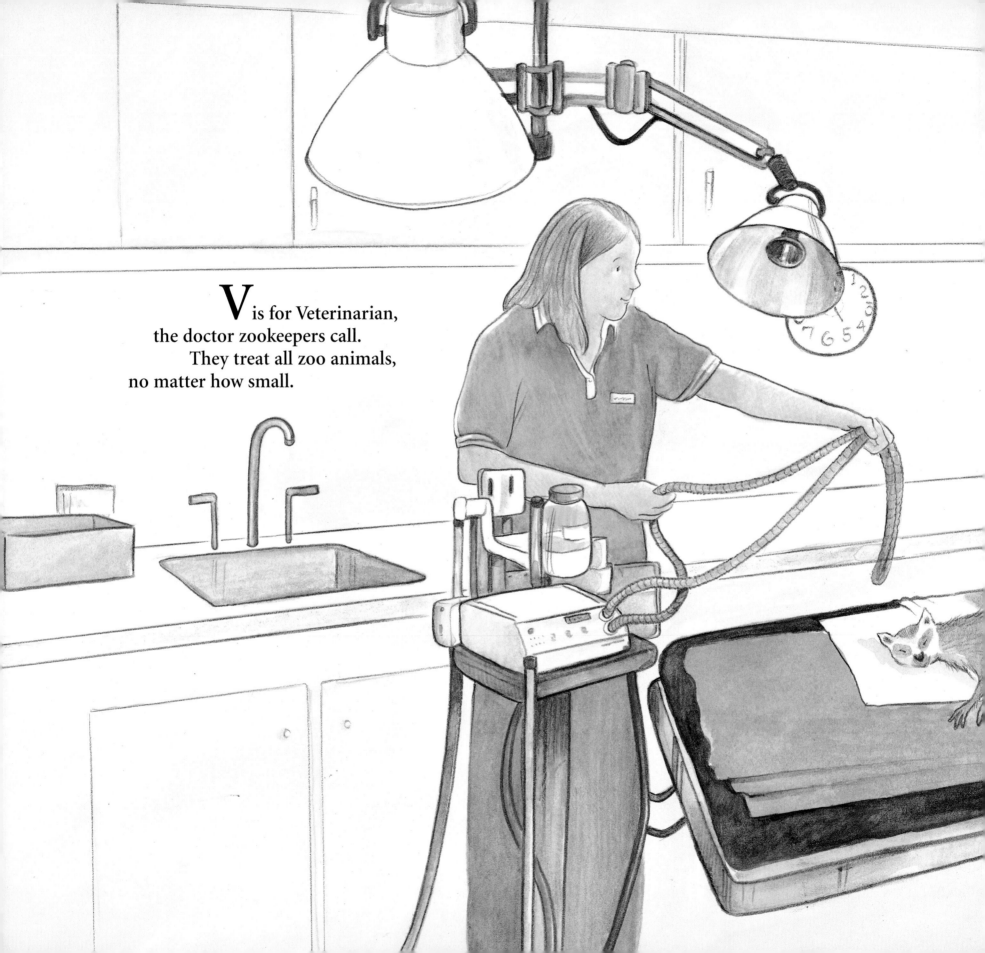

**V** is for Veterinarian,
the doctor zookeepers call.
They treat all zoo animals,
no matter how small.

Most zoos have a full-time veterinarian on staff, or at least a local veterinarian on 24-hour call. You never know when an animal is going to get sick and need medical help.

A zoo veterinarian has to be able to treat animals as big as an 8,000-pound (3,628.7 kg) elephant, or as small as a two-ounce (56.6 g) elephant shrew. This takes a lot of special medical training and years of school.

A big part of the veterinarian's job is preventative medicine. This is stopping diseases and injuries before they affect the animals. They work very closely with the zookeepers, setting up vaccination schedules, vitamin therapy, and husbandry routines.

Red wolves are part of the AZA Species Survival Plan. These distinctive wolves were once found in the southeastern United States in great numbers, but by the mid-1960s the species was nearly extinct, with only a few wolves remaining in Texas and Louisiana. By 1980 the red wolf was found only in zoos. Through the efforts of zookeepers and captive breeding, zoos were able to increase the population to nearly 200 wolves.

In 1987 red wolves were reintroduced into the Alligator River National Wildlife Refuge in North Carolina. Now there are more than 100 red wolves back in the wild.

**W** is for Red Wolves—
    a canine of distinction.
Zookeepers saved them
    from the brink of extinction.

**X** are those things animals leave everywhere. Zookeepers pick them up with the greatest of care.

What do you do with all that poop?

Many zoos turn it into compost, or Zoo Doo. The manure is mixed with straw bedding from animal enclosures. Next, leaves, wood chips, and other organic materials are mixed with the manure and straw. When this is watered and piled into long rows it quickly heats up, reaching 150+ degrees Fahrenheit (65.5°C)! The high temperatures destroy the bacteria and viruses that might cause disease.

The piles are turned and watered until the mixture becomes dark and crumbly, bearing little resemblance to the original poop. After three months the compost is cool and ready for use in home gardens as fertilizer to help plants grow.

X
X

**Y** is for You.
Whether a girl or a boy
a job at the zoo
is one to enjoy.

Being a zookeeper is a great way to make a living. It's a difficult job, but it is never boring. If you want to become a zookeeper you will have to go to college and get a degree in zoology, biology, or wildlife management.

In the meantime, you might want to call your local zoo and ask them about their volunteer programs. Zookeepers love having people come and help them with their work.

In the United States more than 100 million people visit zoos and aquariums every year.

Zoos are not just great places to see animals, they are great places to save animals. When you and your family visit the zoo you are supporting conservation programs, environmental education, and scientific research all over the world.

The next time you go to the zoo, say hello to the zookeepers and don't forget to thank them for the important work they do!

Our alphabet is over
with Z is for Zoo.
Come visit the animals
and the zookeepers, too.

## Marie & Roland Smith

Roland Smith and his wife, author, Marie Smith collaborated on *Z is for Zookeeper: A Zoo Alphabet*. Marie and Roland grew up in Oregon and now live on a small farm south of Portland. Before becoming a full-time writer, Roland spent more than 20 years caring for exotic animals. In his career he has been a zookeeper, senior zookeeper, curator of mammals and birds, general curator, assistant zoo director, and senior research biologist. For many years, Roland was the species coordinator and studbook keeper for the red wolf. In 1980 he was awarded the Excellence in Zoo Keeping award for the United States.

Roland is the author of many award-winning books for children including *Thunder Cave*, *Sasquatch*, *Jaguar*, *The Last Lobo*, *Zach's Lie*, and *The Captain's Dog: My Journey with the Lewis and Clark Tribe*, and *Cryptid Hunters*. Together Marie and Roland also wrote *B is for Beaver: An Oregon Alphabet*; *E is for Evergreen: A Washington Alphabet*; and *N is for our Nation's Capital: A Washington, DC Alphabet*.

## Henry Cole

Before becoming a full-time illustrator and writer, Henry Cole's passion was teaching elementary and middle school science. He has worked on more than 50 books including *Naughty Little Monkeys*, *Jack's Garden*, *On the Way to the Beach*, and *Can You Make a Piggy Giggle?* Henry enjoys gardening, birding, movies, traveling, but most of all, he enjoys illustrating. He now calls Washington, D.C. and the island of Aruba home.